Lillian Candlin

MEMORIES OF
OLD SUSSEX

My sister and myself (on the right) dressed in our 'Sunday Best'.

Lillian Candlin

MEMORIES OF OLD SUSSEX

COUNTRYSIDE BOOKS
NEWBURY, BERKSHIRE

First Published 1987
© Lillian Candlin 1987

All rights reserved. No reproduction
permitted without the prior permission
of the publisher:
COUNTRYSIDE BOOKS
3 Catherine Road
Newbury, Berkshire

ISBN 0 905392 78 7

Cover illustration by kind permission of Tony Wales
Produced through MRM (Print Consultants) Ltd., Reading
Typeset by Acorn Bookwork, Salisbury
Printed in England by J. W. Arrowsmith Ltd., Bristol

Contents

From Adeline —
Summer 1987

Garland Day

'The first of May, is Garland Day,
So please remember the Garland
We don't come here but once a year
So please remember the garland.'

THIS was the song many children sang in the early years of this century, as they paraded through the towns and villages proudly displaying a pole upon which, at the top, was a large bunch of flowers, or a hoop covered with wild flowers, which they called garlands. Some of these were very elaborate and had a doll seated in the centre of crossed hoops.

Garland day was certainly a red letter day for children; in fact it was as exciting as Christmas! In the villages the day was usually an organised affair, with processions, followed by May revels. In the towns the day was kept up in a more individual way.

At Sompting, near Worthing, according to a lady who was born there, the day was a school holiday. But nevertheless, every child assembled at the schoolhouse at the usual time. The girls would have on clean white pinafores, covering, when possible a pretty frock. The boys wore clean collars and their hair was plastered down with so much water that it shone. After much chattering and exciting running to and fro, and a few tears from children whose garlands had been knocked over, a procession was formed and ready to begin its triumphant way through the village.

It was led by the May Queen seated in a donkey cart, and behind came the children carrying nosegays and garlands. Some of the boys carried boughs of blossoming may. These, however, were never allowed inside the schoolhouse, because it was considered unlucky.

By this time all the doors in the village were open and women and children who were too young to attend school, and old people who had left school long ago stood and waved, and dropped a small donation, often a farthing, into the collection boxes as the procession passed by.

The children paraded first to the east, going as far as the Lancing boundary, then back to the western end of the village. In the afternoon the procession was again reformed and the children marched as far as The Marquis of Granby inn, and then turned up the hill to 'Abbots' where May Day revels and a great deal of sport and merriment went on, to end with tea and buns.

Back at the schoolhouse the money that had been collected was distributed and each child, tired but happy, went home with a few coppers wrapped in a screw of newspaper clutched tightly in their hands.

This in itself was exciting because few children in those days ever possessed any money. 'Oh, how we enjoyed garland day!' said my informant with a far away look in her eyes.

A few years ago, a correspondent recounted to the *West Sussex Gazette* her mother's memories of Garland Day at Byworth. Signed W. J. Wood, the letter says that the children of the C.E. school, all carrying garlands and singing 'The first of May etc.' walked with their teachers, Miss Price and Miss Long to Petworth, then to Burton and back to Byworth. The money collected was taken home by the children.

A good description of Garland Day in the early 19th century at Horsham is told by Henry Burstow, in his *Reminiscences of Horsham* published in 1911. This was written in his old age. 'May Day, or Garland Day, was a very jolly time for us youngsters, not only because it was a holiday

Children at Cowfold in 1910 celebrating May Day with their garlands.

but also because we used to pick up what seemed to us quite a lot of money.' Here again it is the money that is remembered as well as the garlands.

This was not an organised affair. Children certainly had a holiday but they went around with a few friends carrying garlands and singing a May song, in front of the big houses and tradesmen's shops. He writes: 'We represented a recognised institution, and were well received and patronised. People all seemed pleased to see us, and we were all pleased to see one another, especially if the weather was fine, as it now seems to me it always was.'

My mother, who was born at Lewes in 1870, went early to

9

the Daisy Bank – a grassy slope opposite the old Fox Inn at Southeram, on the 1st of May to gather wild flowers. Alas! the only wild flowers that grow there now are a few daisies. The flowers were made into a garland which she took around to the neighbours who gave her a penny or a cake for the sight of it.

The streets and the seafront at Brighton right up to the 1930s were brightened by 'May Children'. By that time they were rather bedraggled little groups, shaking money boxes and saying 'Please remember the first of May'.

Far, far different to the May Children who came around when I was a child. They had brightly coloured paper flowers and paper streamers stitched to their clothing and flowers in their hair. The children came around the streets early in the morning in groups of some ten or less. Every so often they stopped in the middle of the road and performed what was obviously the remnants of an old May Day mummers play, and sang what was almost certainly a May Day carol, which had come down by word of mouth until just recently. They began by chanting:

> 'Please remember the first of May,
> It is Our Lady's washing day.
> Say what you will. Say what you may.
> But please remember the first of May.'

Then holding hands in a circle the children walked around singing a song called *All in the twilight underneath the tree*. There were several verses. The first verses go as follows:

> 'All in the twilight underneath the tree,
> There is a sweetheart waiting there for me.
> Tell her that you love her, on your bended knee,
> All in the twilight underneath the tree.
>
> All in the starlight underneath the tree
> There is a sweetheart waiting there for me.
> Tell him that you love him, on your bended knee,
> All in the starlight underneath the tree.'

I have a dim memory that there was a little boy and girl in the centre of the ring.

The song over, the children came up to the doors of the houses rattling their collecting boxes, chanting as they did so:

> 'The first of May is garland day
> The second of May is washing day.
> The third of May is my birthday.
> Hip, hip, hip hurrah!'

The 'my birthday' referred to was probably the Virgin Mary's day in pre Reformation times. The early church leaders dedicated the month of May to Mary to try and kill the pagan memories of the day.

Another type of garland was described to me some time ago by a lady at Lancing. She told how, in the 1920s, she went around with a basket lined with moss, into which sweet-smelling wild flowers were arranged. The garland was covered with a cloth. In return for a penny or a cake, the cloth was lifted to let the giver have a peep at the garland.

Some children, she believed they were the ones who attended the Roman Catholic church, had little dolls nestling among the flowers. These, without a doubt, represented the Virgin Mary.

Garland Day is, of course, another name for May Day, which was one of the most important days in the lives of our pagan ancestors. To them this was the first day of summer, when the sun began to warm up the earth and all things burst into life.

In the Celtic mythological calendar May Day was the feast of Beltane, when Balor, the king of the dead, or Baal, the god of fire was honoured. A character in the Beltane rites was the Green Man, who represented the spirit of the woods, and who could, so it was believed, bring rejuvenation to all things. His image was garlanded with a wreath of May blossom. This was Beltane's sacred tree and it was thought to be scathless, that is a tree too sacred to be touched.

All the pagan rites of May were carried out around the

11

hawthorn tree in full blossom. Later this was superseded by a pole decked with a garland of May flowers. All early maypoles were made of hawthorn wood.

There is a superstition still strongly held among Sussex folk that it is unlucky to bring flowering May into the house. Some say that it means a death in the family. This in all probability is a folk memory that has lingered on from the days of Balor, and his connection with death.

No doubt, the leaders of the early Christian church tried to take away the memory of Beltane by dedicating the month of May to Mary the mother of Jesus, and by so doing spread the superstition by denouncing the hawthorn tree as an evil tree.

There is, however, one good thing remembered about the may tree. This is:

> 'The fair maid who the first of May
> Goes to the fields at break of day
> And washes in dew from the hawthorn tree
> Will ever after handsome be.'

Lucky Stones

MANY people complain that the beaches in Sussex are composed of shingle; they prefer the sand. Children, however, are not so fussy and find much pleasure upon any beach.

One of these pleasures is to hunt for a holed stone – a pebble with a hole right through the centre. This is a lucky stone. The tradition is that the finder should give a big spit through the hole and then throw the stone over their left shoulder. If there is no one sitting behind, this will bring good luck!

In Victorian days children chanted as the stone went over their shoulder. Sir John Evans, in his book *Ancient Stone Implements* says he chanted:

> 'Lucky stone, lucky stone bring me some luck
> Today or tomorrow by 12 o'clock'

P. H. Gosse, however, in *The Aquarium*, written in 1854, says that the chant he knew went:

> 'Lucky stone, lucky, go over my head,
> And bring me some luck before I go to bed'

Sussex fishermen set great store by them. At one time no boat set out for the fishing grounds without a holed stone fixed inside the boat, preferably with a piece of copper wire. This, it was said, protected a man from death by drowning or having his boat capsized.

In the country areas holed stones were hung over the entrances to stables and cowsheds to prevent the animals being 'overlooked', that is being viewed by a witch.

Holed stones also had a reputation of being able to prevent things being stolen. There used to be, and I expect it is still there, a small glass case in South Harting Church in which were some local curiosities. Among them was a little prayer book with a small holed stone fixed to the strip of leather that formed the spine of the book.

During the Second World War, I worked in an accountant's office in Brighton. Here the key of the safe was tied to a holed stone! When I asked the Head Clerk if it was to prevent it being stolen, he answered brusquely 'To stop it getting lost most likely'. He did, however, say that the stone was on the ring when he started working there some fifty years earlier. So who knows!

These stones were sometimes known as 'ague stones'; that is stones that could give protection from catching the dreaded illness known as ague. This complaint was a curse in Victorian days and earlier times. It was mainly due to bad housing. It was certainly more prevalent in country districts that stood along the river valleys.

Ague was a kind of mild typhoid. People suffering from it had high temperatures and shook all over. This meant that sufferers of it were not able to work and that was a terrible thing in the days of 'no work no pay'.

There were numerous old remedies for this. One of these was to hang ague stones in cottage windows and by the side of front doors. I possess two photographs that were taken in 1929 by Mr. Toms, the then curator of Brighton Museum. One shows a bunch of large pebbles, hanging in the front window of a cottage in Southease. Mr. Toms said that the lady of the house told him they were ague stones. The other photo shows a woman standing at a cottage door; hanging on the doorpost is a small holed stone.

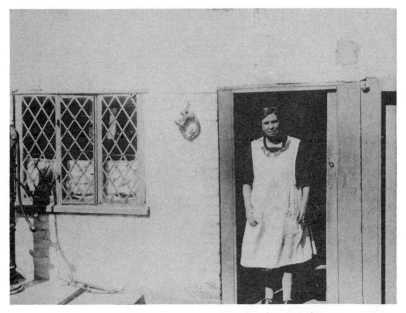

Lucky stones were often hung by cottage doorways, like this one at Beddingham. It was said that they would ward off the 'ague'.

In Victorian times one of the souvenirs taken home by holiday makers at Brighton was a lucky necklace made of holed stones. The stones were fossilised sponges (*Porosphaera globularis*) which at that time could be found in large quantities among the rocks now covered by the Brighton Marina. George Goldsmith remembers that when he worked in Brighton in the 1930s he used to see an old lady named Brown standing with a basketful of these necklaces during the summer months opposite the old chain pier where Volks Electric Railway station now stands. Mrs. Brown used to gather the stones in the winter months, and clean and polish them. She would then thread them onto pieces of ribbon, ready to sell to the summer visitors.

Exactly why holed stones are considered to be so beneficial to their owners is uncertain, but it is thought by many to have an ancient religious significance. There is evidence that these particular stones have had a special meaning in Sussex for thousands of years. Two small holed stones were found in the grave of a Neolithic woman when the Brighton & Hove Archaeological Society excavated a 5000 year old burial site at Whitehawk Hill, Brighton, just beyond the finishing post of the racecourse, in 1922/3.

Professor Margaret Murray, who spent many years studying the religions of early man, gives what is probably the most satisfying explanation. Her theory is that the idea of lucky stones began because the stone looked like an eye – the eye of a great all-seeing spirit. On the tower of the 16th century church of St Mary at Newchurch, Pendle, is a curious carving of a large holed stone, which is known as 'the eye of God'. So the holed stones are thought to relate to the eye of God, and thus bring good fortune on their owners.

Cottage Simples

START on the subject of the simple remedies for illness used in the homes of our parents or grandparents at a Women's Institute Meeting, and there is not a dull moment! Nearly everybody seems to have a memory of a remedy used, and in some cases still used, by their older relatives.

Time and time again I have been told of the Madonna or brandy leaf cure, which at one time was a popular remedy for healing wounds. The petals of the large white garden lily, that in my childhood bordered the gardens of many a cottage, were pressed down tightly, one on top of the other, into a jar of brandy. When needed, a leaf was peeled off and bound onto a cut or wound.

The end of this remedy, without a doubt, was the rise in the price of brandy. One lady who knew of the remedy said that when her mother was preparing it she was sent to the local inn with a request for threepennyworth of brandy!

Marcus Woodward, in his book *The Mistress of Standons* an account of life on a farm near Plumpton about four miles from Lewes, in the early part of the 19th century, says that this was the pet cure of the Mistress. He goes on to explain that the brandy absorbed the flesh of the petals, leaving the skin, which being highly sterilising was effective as a remedy when applied to cuts and festering wounds.

Apparently it was important to apply one side of the petal

to a fresh wound and the other side when it was getting better. A ditty oft quoted when the treatment was being used went:

> 'A leaf of white lily tied on a wound,
> One side heals and the other side draws.'

Sometimes the rhyme says 'the sunny side heals'. So it was evidently important how the leaf was placed on the cut.

In the Parish Book of Rye, for the years 1726–32, there appears this item: 'DR. Hope paid to the poor children of the parish for picking violets, 1s.9d.' Violets were still in use for medicine when I was a child. In fact, the chemist shopkeepers were making a cold cure syrup from violets right up to the Second World War. The chemist where I dealt in Brighton at that time was making it, and I remember him telling me that he had to get a special ration permit from the food office to allow him sugar for the making of it.

Violet Syrup played a large part in my childhood. Whenever colds and coughs appeared in the home, I would be sent with an empty medicine bottle and sixpence to the chemist, and I had to ask for twopennyworth of oil of almonds, twopennyworth of syrup of Violets and two-pennyworth of syrup of squills. It was a delightful tasting medicine. Mother never had any trouble when administering this!

Another use that Dr. Hope may have had for the violets could have been the preparation of cosmetics. This is, perhaps, the greatest use to which violets have been put, both in the past and in the present. Over 1,000 years ago, our Celtic ancestors, according to an ancient Gaelic song, were beautifying their faces with violets. The song says that anyone who annoints their face with goats milk in which violets have been steeped will acquire great beauty. In fact, 'there is no young prince on earth who will not be charmed with your beauty'. Surely no modern advertiser could do better than this!

In the 17th century, violet jam was a popular conserve.

18

King Charles II is said to have been very partial to it. With the amount of kissing of ladies that Charles is reputed to have done, a spoonful of violet jam eaten just before meeting them would have been a great asset. Its virtue was that it made the breath smell sweet.

Another item in the Book of Rye states: 'Dr. Monnoch, to the poor children of the parish for picking primroses. 1s.6d.' A syrup made by boiling primroses with sugar was used as a medicine for insomnia, and all manner of complaints of the nerves, including palsey. Gerarde, the famous herbalist at the time of Queen Elizabeth I, said that primrose tea drunk in the month of May will cure the 'prensie', that is madness.

Cowslips too, played a part in beautifying the ladies of Sussex. I have talked to Sussex women who told how when they were young they tried their grandmothers' recipes for beauty, by boiling cowslips in water for washing their faces. This was thought to make them 'white and ladylike'. This again is an ancient remedy. Our ancestors made cowslips into an ointment by boiling them in wax. Gerarde says that cowslips 'Taketh away the spots and wrinkles of the skin and doth add beauty exceedingly as divers ladies, gentlewomen and she-citizens – whether wives, or widows – know well enough.' (I like the term 'she-citizens'. These, I suppose, were neither 'ladies' or 'paupers'.)

The elder tree has, and still does play, a large part in healing in Sussex, especially in the villages. John Evelyn, the friend of Charles II and a great botanist, called it the medicine plant and wrote of it, 'if the medicine properties of its leaves, bark and berries were fully known, I cannot tell what our countrymen could ail for which he might not fetch a remedy from every hedge either for sickness or wounds'. A view with which I heartily agree. I chew the tiny young leaves, which form just below the blossom, for a laxative. Elder rob, a jam made from the berries is an excellent hot drink for bad colds. Stir a spoonful into a mug of hot water and drink it before getting into bed, and this will 'sweat it out'.

In one period of my life I acted as a leader, a kind of courier, walking parties of ramblers across hills and dales. At a time when a bout of coughs and colds was affecting the party, I stopped by the side of Winchelsea Churchyard, after showing them the church, and insisted that they all chewed elder. Like lambs to the slaughter they chewed, and all agreed that after this their energy returned.

A good old folk cure for ague, and one that was well practised in Sussex where ague was very prevalent, at one time, was to swallow a spider wrapped in its web like a pill. John Wesley who gave advice to his flock for healing bodies as well as their souls, says in a book he published in 1769 on homely remedies: 'For the ague swallow six middling sized pills of cobweb at stated times.'

This is not so far fetched as it sounds for it has been discovered that the tiny hairs of a cobweb contains a substance that is akin to quinine. The old established belief that a cobweb tied over a wound will stop excessive bleeding was in evidence in my childhood. I once saw a butcher at Lewes who had chopped his finger bind it up with a cobweb, dirt and all. Recently there was a report in a local paper of a man being badly cut with a piece of farm machinery arriving at hospital with a spider's web tied on the wound. The doctors admitted that had this not been done the man would have bled to death before reaching the hospital.

In the 15th century, our soldiers at Crècy and Agincourt carried little boxes of webs into battle for the purpose of stopping bleeding. Shakespeare makes Bottom say to Master Cobweb in *A Midsummer Night's Dream*, 'I shall desire you of more acquaintance, good Master Cobweb: If I cut my finger, I shall make bold with you.'

Not only spiders, but frogs, snakes and mice all played a part for healing in our forefathers' time; the principle being that the more noisome the medicine the greater the cure. About a century ago snakes were still being used for curing a goitre in Sussex. At Withyham it was the practice to draw a snake three times across the swelling. The snake was then left to crawl around for a time. This was repeated three times so that the snake was drawn across the neck nine times. It was then put into a tightly sealed bottle and buried in the ground.

As the snake rotted so it was said, the swelling on the neck would gradually die also!

Not quite so bad was the remedy used in a nearby village. Here the dead snake was wrapped in a silk scarf after it had been skinned, and the sufferer had to wear it constantly around her neck until the swelling subsided.

Even more gruesome was the cure reported in the *Brighton Herald* in 1835: 'After the execution a circumstance occurred which excited much surprise that it should have been allowed to occur. This was the ancient and superstitious custom of passing the hand of the dead man while yet warm over the necks of two young females, by whose friends this form is considered as a remedy for diseases of the glands with which they are afflicted.' This took place at Horsham.

Mice for centuries have been used as a remedy for whooping cough. My mother remembered that when she was a child suffering from whooping cough, a neighbour came in and told my mother's mother to boil a mouse in milk and give it to the children. To which her mother replied, 'Mercy on us, Mrs. B——, In these enlightened days?' This was 1880. Richard Stapley, who lived at Hickstead Place in the reign of Queen Anne, wrote a similar remedy in his Diary: 'Take three field mice, flay them, draw them and roast one and let the party afflicted eat it; dry the others in the oven until they crumble to a powder, and put a little of the powder in what the patient drinks at night and in the morning.'

A member of Coolham W.I. told me a few years ago about a health visitor in the Chichester area. One day she had to call at a house about a bed-wetting case. The father opened the door and told her that she need not call any more as they had tried his grandmother's cure and the child was now quite cured. When the health visitor asked him what the remedy was, he replied, 'We boiled a mouse in milk and gave it to the child to drink.'

Shrew mice were worn around a baby's neck in a little bag to aid teething troubles. One lady said she could just remember wearing one.

Many people have told me about a little jar on the mantelpiece behind the clock into which all the odds and end of cheese were dropped. These, when nice and mouldy, were tied onto broken knees. In fact, any wound was said to react to a piece of mouldy cheese.

When one listens to these old wives tales, it makes one wonder whether perhaps Sussex women were not the first to discover penicillin. After all, it is only a mould, isn't it?

Sussex Weather Signs

'To talk of the weather, it's nothing but folly
for when it's rain on the hill it may be sun in the valley.'

NEVERTHELESS, it is a thing we are all guilty of doing, in spite of modern T.V. and radio broadcasts on the weather. When the sun goes red to bed someone is sure to quote:

'Red sky at night is the shepherd's delight,
Red sky at morn is the shepherd's warning.'

This fact was probably even known to Adam. It was certainly used by Christ some two thousand years ago, for did he not say when the Pharisees and Sadducees asked him for a sign: 'When it is evening, ye say: "It will be fair weather for the sky is red". And in the morning "It will be foul weather today for the sky is red and lowering".' Whether this ditty will be quoted in another two thousand years, who knows? By then the weather may be decided by a computer or some such thing.

My earliest recollections of forecasting the weather is of trailing home from the beach (I lived by the sea) with a long piece of smelly seaweed. My mother must have been very long-suffering. How many mothers, today, would hang a piece of high smelling seaweed in her modern kitchen so that her children could give it a pinch each morning to see whether it was wet or dry? I might add that the craze only lasted for a few days.

Another early memory is of having a little wooden house, with two doors. Inside of one stood a little wooden man and in the other a little wooden lady. If the man came out it was going to rain, but should the lady step outside then it would be dry.

There are many weather sayings remembered in Sussex. An old rhyme quoted in Brighton goes:

'When the island's seen above the line,
Brighthelmstone loses weather fine.'

I have lived in Brighton all my life and only once have I seen the Isle of Wight from Brighton beach. This was in the middle of a hot, dry spell in 1937. The island could be seen that year from the Brighton racecourse.

In the neighbourhood of Steyning, people look to Chanctonbury Ring for their local weather lore. If the ring of trees on the top is hidden in a mist it means that rain is coming, for the saying known here is:

'Old Mother Goring's got her cap on,
We shall have some wet.'

Chanctonbury is sometimes known as Goring, because it was one of the Goring family of Wiston House who planted the ring of trees in 1760.

On washing days it was important for Sussex women to forecast a good drying day. The women of Lewes were once said to take a look at Beddingham hill. The people of Alciston looked to Firle Beacon and those who lived at Romney Marsh also looked to the hills.

'When Beddingham hills wears a cap
Ripe and Chalvington get a drap.'

'When Firle Hill and Long Man has a cap
Romney Marsh will have a sap.'

24

Sussex shepherds knew many rhymes and sayings for prophesying the weather.

In the Weald around Ditchling way it is said 'It is going ter rain; Wolstonbury's got her nightcap on.'

Cocking in West Sussex has a way all its own of deciding on what the weather is going to do, by watching 'foxes-brewings'. This is a thick mist-like smoke which when the weather is unsettled lies among the thick leafy beech trees hanging on the sides of the Downs. If foxes-brewings turn towards Cocking, rain will soon appear. But if the mist rises slowly straight up the hill it is a sign of a hot day or a spell of hot weather. Here the saying is:

> 'When foxes-brewings go to Cocking,
> Foxes-brewings come home dropping.'

25

A weather sign to the fishermen of Hastings is when they can hear the 'bells of Bulverhythe'. The bells is a raking sound made by the sea in the bay to the west of St. Leonards.

Similarly the fishermen of Brighton say that when the sea washes the shingle up the beach into scallop shapes at the high tide mark, the town is in for a storm. The scallop shapes are just what they say, long hollows in the shingle.

The explanation of this, according to the fishermen, is that when there is a bad storm further down the coast to the west, the underwater of the sea gets to Brighton before the top. Whether this is the correct cause, I am not knowledgeable enough to know, but it is true that a storm does often follow when this scalloped shingle occurs.

Some years ago when up on Chanctonbury hill, the then local shepherd, whose name I think was Styles, told me to get down home as there was rain coming. When I asked him how he knew with such certainty, he pointed to his sheep, and said: 'See my old ship (sheep) — they all be turned with their tails to the wind. They knows as rain is a'coming.' My grandmother had two sayings about what she considered to be sure signs of coming rain. One was 'Leaves of the trees blowing backward upwards'; and the other was: 'The cat sleeping on its brains.' When the wind blows the leaves so that the underside shows, is one of the surest of signs and one that I take note of and make for home.

Now that you know the rainy signs of Sussex, you have no one to blame but yourself if you go out unprepared and get a soaking!

The Magic
Good Friday Bun

'Hot cross buns! Hot cross buns!
One a penny, two a penny, hot cross buns.
If you have not any daughters give them to your sons,
If you have not any sons then God Bless You.'

THIS was a ditty chanted every year as Good Friday came around.

In the 1920s the bakers' boys came around the streets of Brighton early in the morning crying their wares of 'Hot Cross Buns!' The buns then were really hot, having just come out of the oven. At that time bakers worked all night baking bread for their next day's trade.

On Good Friday as soon as the last batch of bread came out from the oven, trays loaded with spicy buns were popped in. The buns only took a few minutes to cook and then out they all came crisp and brown. A quick brush of sugar water over the tops to make them shine, and the buns were ready to be packed into paper bags for the waiting errand boys to start their rounds.

In those days hot cross buns were all baked in local bakehouses, which were then to be found in all the shopping centres. In St James' Street, Brighton, there were five bakehouses, all within a stone's throw of each other. Up from the gratings under the shops would come a warm, mouthwatering smell of newly baked bread and spicy buns. A heady aroma that today's children cannot even imagine.

It is a staggering thought that buns could then be bought for a halfpenny (old money). Large buns were sold at a penny each, and most bakers threw in an extra bun when six were bought, hence seven small buns for threepence or seven large for sixpence.

Hot cross buns were known to older folk in those days as Good Friday buns. My grandmother always referred to them as such. She used to say that many people thought they were a kind of magic bun, endowed with all manner of powers which were thought to go back to the time before Sussex became Christian.

Some of this magic still held sway up to the early years of this century. I remember as a very small child seeing a bun on a long piece of string (I believe it was red string) hanging by the side of an old fashioned high kitchen mantelpiece. This, I was told by the old lady that lived there, was to preserve the house from being harmed by fire or tempest, and it was also thought that it would bring blessings in the shape of peace and happiness.

This woman had baked a bun on Good Friday throughout all the years of her married life, being always careful to mark the bun with a cross, which she did by laying two strips of pastry crossways on top.

A Miss French, a native Sussex woman who lived at Selsey, recalled that when her great uncle Morris died (he was a shoemaker at Bognor at the end of last century), a row of buns was found in the house. Each one of them was labelled with the date that the bun had been baked.

Sometimes, however, it was little loaves of bread baked on a Good Friday that were hung by the hearth. A lady at Horsham once told me about an aunt of hers, who up to the year of her death at the age of 80, baked three little loaves to

28

hang by her fireplace every Good Friday. After her death the three loaves were found hanging there.

Some villagers used to hang a bun outside their front door. This was said to keep witches and suchlike evil spirits out. Sussex fishermen were known at one time to carry one of these buns in their pocket when they went to sea, in the belief that no man could die by drowning if he had a Good Friday bun on him.

Mothers of young children set great store by having a Good Friday bun in the house. This, it was thought was capable of giving immunity to children from whooping cough, one of the greatest killers of children a hundred years ago. The buns in this case were not hung up but kept in a box or bag, one for each child on the first Good Friday after its birth. A district Nurse who had to visit a cottage to bring a baby into the world during World War II, said she noticed a paper bag pinned up over the fireplace in the bedroom. When she asked what was in the bag, she was told that the bag contained hot cross buns, to keep fevers away.

At Aldingbourne, during a discussion on homely cures, a lady stood up and told the audience that when her mother died, she found in a drawer a little box that contained three little hard round objects which turned out to be three very stale hot cross buns. She said with a chuckle, 'But I believe all three of us children caught the whooping cough'.

Another strong belief about these buns was that no matter how long they were kept they would never go mouldy. There used to be a ditty quoted in my school days that went:

> 'Good Friday comes and the old woman runs,
> With one a penny, two a penny, Hot Cross Buns.
> Whose virtue is, if we believe what is said,
> They'll not grow mouldy like the common bread.'

Whether Good Friday buns and bread did go mouldy, is of course, open to question, but it must be likely that the tops of the sticky buns would sometimes go mouldy, especially during the wet weather in damp cottages.

My father's shop in St James Street, Brighton. This picture was taken in the 1940s.

If this did happen it gives some point to the practice women had of using the bun to cure the stomach-ache. When any member of the family complained of this, the bun was taken down from its piece of string and a little of it was grated into a mug of hot water which the sufferer had to drink. Farmers, in the past, have been known to have used this remedy to cure cattle when they had the murrain.

This was probably an early use of the bacterical properties

30

of the fungus *Penicillium notatum* (*perispopiaceae*) otherwise penicillin, although in those days it was regarded as just an 'old wives tale'. It might have been just an old wives tale but it goes to show that many of these homely remedies did in fact have some scientific basis to them.

Folk Cures for
An Ampre-Ang

AMPRE-ANG is Sussex dialect for a decaying or aching tooth. The word was often heard in my young days when children came to school with badly swollen faces tied up in a large handkerchief – often a red one. In folk medicine the colour red was always thought to be beneficial.

To-day, however, due to the National Health Service, toothache, the curse of our ancestors for thousands of years, has practically disappeared. Prior to this the visit to a dentist was a luxury that many people could not afford. Consequently numerous folk cures were in use.

These ranged from plants found in garden and hedgerow to paper amulets worn around the neck. One amulet particularly popular in Sussex, so it is claimed, had these curious words written on it: 'As Peter sat weeping on a "marvel" stone, Christ came by and said unto him: "What ailest thee Peter?" Peter said: "Lord I have the toothache so bad that I can neither walk, lie or stand". Jesus said "Arise Peter and be thou whole: and not only thee, but all them that carry these lines for my sake shall never have the toothache any more."'

Many a tale has been told to me of a character called Sequah, the 'painless tooth extractor', who used to travel around the country some 100 years ago, selling an elixir for the prevention and cure of toothache. One lady, a Mrs. Diplock of Brighton, described to me an eye witness account of this man at work a century ago, on an open piece of ground in Seaside road, at Eastbourne. 'As he yanked out the teeth he threw them gaily over his shoulder, while a pipe organ blared out his signature tune *Has anyone here seen Sequah?*'

My dentist in the 1940s, a Mr. Lewery, who had a surgery in Queens Road, Brighton, used to tell with a chuckle of how, as a boy he had seen this man at work on an open space at the top of North Road in Brighton which was later covered by the Grand Theatre. He described Sequah as an outstanding personality, tall, well built, with flowing white hair, white moustache, and goatee beard. He dressed in a flamboyant wild west outfit of brown leather fringed jacket, white buckskin breeches and shiny black thigh-length boots with silver spurs. He carried a whip with a short stock and very long thong. This he cracked expertly over the head of any individual in the crowd.

Before starting to work he set up a platform in front of his horse-drawn caravan. This was painted with vivid pictures of Red Indians in full war paint. When he had attracted a large crowd, Sequah would offer to pull teeth out painlessly and free of charge. As soon as some half dozen volunteers were up on the platform Sequah began. First he set the pipe organ going inside the caravan, at top speed, to drown the cries of his victims.

Suddenly he would stop and look with horror into the mouth of one of his captives, and in a loud voice he began to describe the terrible diseased state of the man's mouth and what this would do to his bodily health. All of which could be averted if the man took Sequah's Elixir, a bottle of which he then gave to the man free of charge. At the psychological moment while people were moving their tongues around to see if their teeth were in the same state, Sequah would produce his bottles of Elixir and at sixpence a bottle they sold like hot cakes.

33

It is hard to realise today that until the opening years of this century many people went to a chemist's shop to get their teeth pulled out. My grandfather used to tell of his one and only visit to have a tooth pulled out – this would have been in the 1880s – and he would point out to us children where this took place. It was in a chemist's shop on the north side of the Cliff High Street, at Lewes. According to grandfather, the man told him to come into the room behind the shop, where he proceeded to put a 'gurt old tool' into grandfather's mouth. He gave a pull. Grandfather gave a yell, and leaping out of the chair, he shouted 'I'll keep the tooth', and keep it he did. At 80 years of age he could still crack nuts with his own teeth.

Earlier still it was the local blacksmith who did the teeth extracting. Even Royalty did not despise the skill of these men. In January 1809, George, Prince of Wales, was attacked with a bout of toothache as he was about to depart from his Brighton Pavilion for his London Palace. So bad was the pain that his advisors suggested that he sent for a local blacksmith, by name Teddy Palmer, who owned a forge in George Street, only a stone's throw from the Pavilion.

This man, George was told, had invented a new cure for toothache which is much acclaimed. This impressed George and he gave the order that the man should be sent for. Teddy Palmer arrived in very quick time. According to a report in the *Brighton Herald*, he arrived still in his sooty clothes but with his hands and face as clean as soap and water could make them.

On arrival Palmer set up his apparatus, which consisted of a small iron box, covered with a tight-fitting lid to which was attached a long tube with a funnel on the end of it. He also had a small spirit stove. He put the box over the stove and when it was well-heated he dropped in a few seeds, fixed the lid on tightly and left it for a while over the stove.

The Prince was then requested to put the funnel into his mouth and to breath in the fumes and work them around his mouth. After only four minutes, according to the report, the Prince's condition was changed from a state of extreme torture to complete ease. A further treatment next morning completed the cure, and the Prince was able to set out for London in good spirits.

Was Palmer using the old London mountijacks 'cure' and using henbane seeds, which are painkillers, to simply temporarily deaden the pain of the aching tooth? This is quite probable. *The Brighton Herald*, published a week or so later a letter written by Palmer, saying that the rumour now being spread around the town that the Prince's tooth began to ache again before he reached Burgess Hill, was a scandalous and malignant libel.

Blacksmiths continued to pull teeth until well into Victoria's reign, but by the middle of the 19th century the task had fallen to the apothecary.

Folk cures were still in use right up to the days of the Second World War. My mother's standby was an onion. An onion was put in the oven until it was 'piping' hot, that is heated right through but not yet soft. The centre piece of the onion was quickly pushed out, and one or two cloves poked into it. This was then laid as hot as the sufferer could bear it, into the mouth against the aching tooth. I can personally vouch that this treatment often worked. Sometimes just a piece of raw onion was used.

Essence of cloves was a well-used remedy in a lot of homes. It is safe to say that fifty years ago most medicine cupboards housed a small bottle of it. To work this cure the gums around the bad tooth were painted with a piece of cotton wool that had been dipped in essence of cloves. People who could not afford essence of cloves made do with a couple of cloves stuck into a piece of bread that had been soaked in boiling water, and those who could not afford the cloves made do with just a small piece of bread soaked in hot water. One man said to me that he rubbed his gums with garlic, which no doubt kept his relatives at a safe distance.

Hurrah for the National Health Service!

The Sussex Tipteerers

TIPTEERERS is the Sussex name for a party of mummers. Every Sussex town and village, at one time, had its band of tipteerers who went around at Christmas and at other festivals performing the play *The Seven Champions of Christendom*. It is a tale about St George of England and his fight against the heathens.

The play is known in many parts of Britain. It is thought to have been part of a miracle play of the Middle Ages. The earliest printed copy appeared in 1596, and at that time, the collector, Richard Johnson, wrote that it was 'already traditional'.

The text of the play has become much changed over the years, so that the words vary from village to village. This is not surprising, since it was passed down by word of mouth from one generation of players to the next and its accuracy depended on the memory of the man who was passing it on. The first written copy of the Sussex version was not made until the middle of the 19th century.

In recent years the Sussex Morris Men have revived the play, and they go around performing it on Boxing Day. Today it is an accepted part of the Christmas jollifications,

The Shoreham Tipteerers celebrating May Morning.

and is performed with the stress on comedy. Some do feel, and I am among them, that nowadays some of the point of the play is being missed, however, by concentrating on the hilarious episodes. We tend to forget now that for the traditional tipteerers in bygone times the play had a deep spiritual meaning, symbolising the death and resurrection of the good earth. They therefore performed it with a more befitting dignity.

George Attrill, that grand old man who many West Sussex folk will remember for his folk singing, got together a party of men in the 1930s who went round performing the play to make a little extra money for Christmas in those hard times.

George, a keen member of the Sussex branch of the English Folk Song and Dance Society, offered to perform the play at a weekend conference at Lodge Hill, Pulborough in 1948 which I was fortunate enough to see.

Before the play started, George, who was a stickler for seeing that the play should be performed in the traditional way, gave a short talk about it. He made it quite clear that it was a symbol of the death and resurrection of the good earth. He also said that at the end of the play there would be a collection but this was only being done so that the tradition would not be broken, and that we should only put in a small coin such as a halfpenny.

George also insisted that every performance must end with a carol. Carols were traditionally very important. One band of Sussex tipteerers had an extra character, whose sole purpose was to exort all those present to sing. Known in some tipteerer performances as the Prince of Peace, he came forward at the end, and said:

'For at this time all blood and warfare must cease.
Peace ladies and gentlemen, let your voices ring.
Clap your hands together and let us sing.'

Incidentally, it is interesting that today there is a revival of the practice of clapping hands. At many carol services recently young people have spontaneously started clapping.

The most popular carol with the tipteerers was the lovely one *The Moon Shines Bright*, which begins:

'The moon shines bright,
and the stars give a light,
A little before the day;
Our mighty Lord He looked on us,
And bade us awake and pray.'

There were four verses, and the last one gives a blessing to the onlookers, no doubt, with an eye on the money box, then going the rounds:

'My song is done, I must be gone,
I stay no longer here,

38

God bless you all both great and small
And send you a joyful New Year.'

The Compton tipteerers in the early years of this century sang *I Saw Three Ships Come Sailing In*, sometimes known as *As I Sat On A Sunny Bank*. The first verse gave tidings of their arrival:

'As we come out on Christmas Day, Christmas Day,
  Christmas Day
As we come out on a Christmas Day, So early in the
  morning.'

From the third verse and the fourth verse, one can understand the orthodox Christian's objection, in Victorian times, to these carols being included in hymn books. Carols found no place in the hymn books of any religious denomination at one time, and were always sung from carol sheets.

It is hard to imagine our Victorian ancestors singing the following words in Church or Chapel:

'He did whistle and She did sing
And all the bells of heaven did ring,
For Christ our Saviour he was born
On Christmas Day in the morning.'

The final verse is quite secular:

'Jack was nimble and Jack was quick.
Jack jumped over the candlestick.
Jack was nimble and Jack was quick,
On Christmas Day in the morning.'

This verse refers to the sword or morris dance which was performed at some period in the play. Some years ago a particular party of Tipteerers I was watching ended with a solo performance of the Fool's Jig.

We owe a great debt to the Tipteerers and other Mummers who went around keeping the traditional mummers play and the folk carols alive. But for them, many of the carols which are now such a part of the Christmas festivities would have been completely forgotten.

Midsummer
Memories

THERE are all kinds of traditions and superstitions associated with the celebration of Midsummer's Eve in Sussex, many of which were widely observed when I was young.

On Midsummer's Eve the Celts celebrated the festival of the Sun God, and up on the Downs great sacrificial bonfires were lit to his honour. Later, the night became one of magic and mystery, when witches, fairies and ghostly apparitions were abroad.

Right up to the time of the Tudors, there was a common belief that on this one night of the year the dead could come back and walk around the earth until cockcrow. Hence the many stories about ghostly visitors on Midsummer's Eve.

At a meeting of the Brighton and Hove Archaeological Society some years ago, the archaeologist S. S. Frere was giving a lecture about an excavation of the site of a Roman Villa and Temple, by the side of the track which leads from North Lancing to Lancing Clump. Suddenly Mr. Frere stopped his talk and remarked, with a twinkle in his eye, that there was a local tradition that anyone who came and stood on this spot at midnight on Midsummer's Eve would hear the sound of ghostly horses going by.

This folk memory may go back to the time when horses dragged great vessels full of water along this track for use in the Roman Camp on Cissbury. Certainly, a memory remains in the district that water for the camp was fetched from a spring, known as Ladywell, on Applesham Farm in the valley north of Lancing College. After passing the site of the Roman Villa, this track runs across the slope of Steepdean direct to Cissbury.

At Broadwater, Worthing, there is a memory that from beneath an old oak tree which stands at the north-east corner of Broadwater Green, a group of skeletons rises up on Midsummer's Eve, and proceeds to dance around the tree to music made by the rattling of their bones. There are now two oak trees growing on this spot. I asked an elderly man sitting on a seat close by whether he knew which was the tree the skeletons danced around. He answered without the slightest hesitation, as he pointed to the largest of the trees, that he believed it was that one. It is nice to think that the memory still survives.

This is a tale that may have its origin in some rite that was practised here many years before the Romans came. Our early Celtic ancestors worshiped the oak tree, and the site of this tree is almost opposite the end of an ancient track which to this day is a footpath that descends to Broadwater from Cissbury.

A few years ago, the vicar of All Saints Church, Hove, wrote an article for the Parish Magazine of a curious tale about Midsummer's Eve, that had been told to him by an elderly verger. It concerned a magic way which once ran from Sackville Road to Hollingbury Camp, via Old Shoreham Road, the Droveway, Millers Road, Robertson Road and Surrender Road.

The story goes that anyone who begins to walk along this route from the Hove end on Midsummer's Eve will find that as soon as they set foot in Hollingbury Ring they will find themselves back on the spot that they started from. The verger asserted that he had personally experienced this.

The route, without a doubt, was at one time an ancient

trackway that led from Goldstone Bottom, where a pagan circle once stood, to Hollingbury Iron Age Camp. (The Godstone that now stands in Hove Park is said to have once been part of this henge.) The magic way in all probability was therefore the way that the early people living in Hollingbury Camp travelled to their place of worship. Midsummer's Eve would certainly have been one of the days that they would have walked the track, in order to be inside the henge when the sun rose on Midsummer's Day.

The story of their being transported back to the place from which they had come could be a memory of the special bonfires lit on that night. When the fire was lit at Goldstone Bottom it would have immediately been taken up by the watchers at Hollingbury, and the bonfire there would have been seen to burst into flame.

Because of the belief that the dead could come back on this night and take possession of anybody that was asleep, many special plants were grown and came into use on Midsummer's Eve. When I was in my teens the plant that flourished in many a Sussex cottage garden was Live-long-love-long (*Sedum telephium*). On Midsummer's Night boys went around with a sprig of it pushed through the moon of their caps. It was believed by them that this would help them in their courting.

Schoolgirls made 'midsummer men' to find out if their boy friends were true or false. Two sprigs of this plant were stuck into the tops of two empty cotton reels. These were set up on the bedroom mantelpiece at bedtime. One reel was given the name of the boyfriend of the moment, and the other reel represented themselves. If by morning the sprigs had bent over towards each other then all was well. On the other hand should the sprigs have fallen away from each other, then it was time to look for a new boy friend.

Bunches of this plant were picked on this night and hung up in attic or spare room to dry. At Christmas time the sprigs were put among the decorations, in the belief that this would bring to the home health and happiness during the coming year.

Another plant that was much in evidence on this night was St John's Wort (*Hypericum perforatum*). This was the plant that could keep witches at bay, and any other evil thing that might be abroad on this night. When I was young, an older girl gave me a sprig of St. John's wort, complete with its bright yellow flower, and told me to pin it on my nightgown as it would keep the witches away. The night, I might add, was Midsummer's Eve. Apparently, even the smell of this plant is abhorrent to witches; the faintest whiff being enough to send them packing!

In pre-Christian days this was Baldur's plant, but when Christianity arrived here, the early church leaders altered the name to St. John's wort, after St. John the Baptist. In spite of its new name, however, people still remembered the powers of Baldur, and, 'just in case', continued to wear the plant on Midsummer's night.

Mugwort (*Artemisia vulgaris*), was perhaps the plant most in evidence on this night. It was said to possess very potent powers for keeping the spirits of the dead who were wandering around on this night from taking possession of anyone who had fallen asleep. This plant, along with St. John's wort, was worn by all. Wreaths of it were hung on front doors and trails of the plant were entwined around doors, window frames and bed-posts.

Gerarde, in his *Herbal*, written in the reign of Elizabeth I, tells how the poor women of the village of Whitechapel carried many tons of mugwort, which they had gathered from the marshes there, to London, for sale in the various markets on Midsummer's Eve.

Mugwort is an example of 'how is the mighty fallen'. Few people who live in towns now even know what it looks like, though anyone who is interested to find out can see a bed of it growing in the herb garden of Rudyard Kipling's one-time home at Rottingdean. But it is fascinating that so much folk lore to do with this special night has survived the passage of the centuries from pre-Christian days to the present time.

Fair Gingerbread

EGDEAN, a village near Petworth, had a fair that was held in the month of May. In 1796, it was overwhelmed by a storm of rain. A local paper reported: 'All the gingerbread sellers sustained considerable losses as canvas coverings were by no means proof against the excessive hasty showers which made such havoc among the kings and queens'. The 'kings and queens' would have been gingerbread ones, which were a popular fairing (i.e. a present or gift bought at a fair) for many years.

It was considered lucky to eat a piece of fair gingerbread, and all who visited a fair either ate a piece of gingerbread or took some home in the shape of a fairing for those who had had to stay at home. Gingerbread fairings were either little effigies, or squares of gingerbread with a pattern stamped on top. By the 19th century this patterning had arisen to great heights, and the pictures of expensive cakes, priced at sixpence or a shilling were painted with Dutch gold – hence the saying 'To take the gilt off the gingerbread'.

The wooden moulds that were used for stamping gingerbread are now museum pieces, and the patterns they portray are almost a history in themselves. They vary from the symbol of the type of fair – a lamb for a sheep fair; horns for a horn fair; knots-in-May (a May posy) for May-day fairs; and so on, to topical events.

Brighton Museum possesses a goodly collection of these moulds. There is the Duke of Wellington on horseback, all complete with sword and pistol; a solemn looking cat, and a grandfather clock. There is also a strange looking creature, rather like a cock sitting on a nest in the shape of a pair of trousers. This mould was once used by A. Chatfield of Horsham, when he was making gingerbread for sale at one of Horsham's many fairs.

Mayhew, writing in Victorian times, described this patterning as 'a formidable-looking bird with his nether garments gilded'.

In Brighton, at the time of the Regency, a popular mould was the Prince of Wales' feathers, all a-curl. There is a mould in the Brighton museum collection of this design that was once used by Mr. Hooker, of Edward Street, Brighton. Some older residents will remember him, or at least remember a shop of that name, which stood on the site of what is now County Court.

There is also a mould of the Royal Arms that belonged to Mr. Streeter, the man who opened the first Old Bun Shop, which still stands in Pool Valley, Brighton, but now closed.

There are other moulds from Horsham, where at one time there were ten bakers' shops, all of which had men working long hours at fair time just baking gingerbread.

The shops were kept by Abraham Chatfield, Bishopric; Harry Chatfield, East Street and West Street; William Hull, West Street; Thomas Richardson, East Street; Alfred Leader, Queens Street; Tom Foreham, Queens Street; George Lovekin, 36 London Road; Thomas Dendy, Church Causeway; Thomas Burstow, Brighton Road, and Sidney Ansell, West Street.

The moulds were square and of a standard size, and acted as measures because the law was very strict on the weight and quality of the cakes; in fact, they came under the same regulations as bread.

The moulds were pressed upon the unbaked dough and each piece was cut off level with the mould. A special palette

A mould used to stamp patterns on little squares of
gingerbread which were sold at fairs.

knife was used for doing this and it had to be wiped clean
after each cake had been cut.

Shelley the poet, when a small boy of nine years of age, was
apparently very fond of Horsham gingerbread. On the 18th
of July 1803, he wrote to a friend at Horsham. The letter
ends, 'Tell the bearer not to forget to bring me a fairing,

47

which is some gingerbread, sweetmeat, hunting nuts, and a pocket book.'

Another kind of gingerbread, or rather ginger biscuit, popular at fairs was known as Parliament. This was a straw coloured biscuit with crinkled edges, rather like an outsize *petit buerre* biscuit.

Parliament could be bought at Brighton in the Old Bun Shop until the Second World War, but when rationing of bread and flour came into operation the baking of Parliament had to stop. Up to that time it was sold at two biscuits for 1½d (old money).

The biscuits were stored in tall glass jars with dome shaped lids. One of the joys of buying Parliament was to watch the lady assistant lift the lid and take the biscuits out with her fingers. None of those new-fangled tongs in those days.

Why, one wonders has the popularity of gingerbread waned in recent years? For centuries it was popular and eaten at all religious festivals. Originally fairs were held on the eve, day, and morrow of the saint to whom the local church was dedicated. How or why gingerbread became connected with religious festivals has never been entirely clear. It is significant, however, that the use of ginger is not only found in Christian countries. In the Philippines ginger was believed to have the power of driving out evil spirits which brought disease. The Polynesians built the roof over their altars with ginger leaves; the Melanesians used ginger when making love-potions; and the North-American Indians believed that wild ginger cooked with bad meat would protect them from ptomaine poisoning.

At today's fairs, alas, candy floss and toffee apples, hamburgers and hot dogs have superseded the traditional lucky piece of gingerbread.

Sussex as She is Spoke

IN my early days Sussex was rich with its own grammar and dialect. All words that ended in 'st' were given a double plural. At that time there was a popular ditty often quoted by parents and teachers in an effort to check this fault. It went:

'I saw three ghosteses' sitting on posteses.
Eating hot toasteses.
The butter ran down their fisteses.
Dirty little beasteses.'

In the spring of 1980 I was standing at a bus stop near Ringmer. Waiting along with me was a countryman. As is usual with such men he started a conversation. To my delight, he said 'Days be drawing out.' then pointing to a tree he continued 'I sees the birdies be building their nesteses.' I could have hugged him! It was wonderful to hear again someone speaking my Sussex.

The double plural was also added to pronouns. In the 1930s I taught in a Brighton Sunday School which was situated in a neighbourhood where a lot of fishermen and their families lived. When it was time to take the collection the younger children walked around a table singing and dropping their farthings into a bowl. The song was:

My grandparents. Grandmother, a Sussex woman born and bred, was very knowledgeable about the county's dialect.

'Hear the pennies dropping.
Listen to them fall.
Everyone for Jesus,
He shall have them all.'

After the children were all again in their seats, I asked 'Have you all put your money in?' A small girl shot up her hand and said: 'Useses 'as put oureses in 'as'nt us Miss?' (I have put mine in, have I not Miss).

The Anglo-Saxon form of hime, thine, hisn, hern, ourn, yourn, and theirn was also to be heard. A saying quoted to children if they were suspected of helping themselves to a sweet or biscuit, went:

'He that takes what isn't hisn
When he's caught will go to pris'n.'

50

My grandmother spoke the dialect and, although my mother did not, many dialect words were in constant use in our home.

'Leer', was used for hungry. We would slap ourselves in the middle and say we were leer. The hitting of our stomachs is significant as in old German, leer is the word for empty.

'Schmosell' was the word used if we got too noisy. 'Don't make such a schmosell' or 'You never heard such a schmosell.'

'Shay' was a word used for many things. It meant a kind of gleam or glimmer, but no word gives quite the right idea. For instance when the moon has a mist around it this is described as a shay. People when choosing dress or upholstery material, such as silk or satin, would say 'It has a nice shay about it'. During a storm you may not have seen the lightning, but you saw the shay of it.

Ghosts were said to have shays around them. Parish, in his *Dictionary of Sussex Dialect*, 1875, tells of a man who was frightened by a ghostly white horse dashing past him, and he described it as having a shay around it.

'Ban-yan day' was a day when left-overs from a celebration or party were forming the ingredients of a meal. I can see my mother now, with her carving knife and fork held ready saying 'It's ban-yan day today, what will you have?' All through the years we wondered where it came from. In fact, some of the family thought that Mother invented the name.

Imagine my surprise, therefore, when visiting Kentucky, in the U.S.A., to find the word in a *A Treasury of Southern Folklore* by B. A. Botkin. He was describing 'burgoo' a traditional dish, a kind of huge stew-cum-soup, which contained flesh, fowl and good red herring, and at one time was popular with hunters and fishermen. The word burgoo he says, was used by English-speaking sailors for thick oatmeal porridge, and goes on to say that a verse of a 19th century British song mentions ban-yan. The verse is as follows:

'They put me to mess with some of the crew,
They called it ban-yan day and gave me burgoo.'

'Afore' is often used for before. In East Dean, in East Sussex, Dan, a gardener, used it and when he said it in rich Sussex dialect is sounded marvellous. Dan also had the Sussex wit. One day when I was starting out for a country walk the weather looked 'quizzby' (unsettled) and I asked Dan if it was going to rain. 'Well', he replied, 'it won't rain afore you gets back.' It poured with rain, and when I got back I said to him: 'You said it was not going to rain.' 'No, I didn't, I said it wouldn't afore you got back, but you didn't get back soon enough.'

At Selsey, I was told by a Miss French who had been born there about the term 'cough I lay'. During the Second World War their gardener, who was then in his 85th year, came out carrying a great scythe when he saw a German parachuting down during the great Tangmere raid. He said 'This'll make the so-and-so cough I lay'.

A common error in Sussex speech is 'off of'. In spite of my parents and schoolteachers constant saying 'You can't get off "of" anything. You get off', I still find myself using it.

Since visiting Kentucky, U.S.A., I have been consoled. There the term is considered correct. So now instead of speaking bad grammer I speak American!

But wouldn't it be a shame if the Sussex dialect and speech mannerisms died out altogether. Long live 'Sussex as she is spoke'!

No Play on Sunday

IN the early years of this century the following song was taught to small children, and it gives a good idea of how Sunday was regarded by many people in Brighton up to the outbreak of the First World War in 1914.

'I must not play on Sunday, because it is a sin.
But when it comes to Monday then I may begin.
Oh! I can play on Monday, Tuesday, Wednesday,
Thursday, Friday and Saturday, till Sunday comes again.'

Sunday was a day of no play and, for many adults, no work. Very few shops opened on this day, although on the piers the bands played and the stalls were opened for the visitors.

There was also a row of shops in Madeira Road, which were nothing more than lean-to sheds built against the wall of the cliff between the east end of the old Aquarium and the first flight of steps up to the Marine Parade, which opened. They sold sweets, fruit, lemonade and ginger beer, and sometimes, when the owners had time to make it, ice cream in penny cornets.

Near here an Italian sold hokey-pokey, from a handcart that was distinctive, in that these types of carts were made

In Edwardian times, Sunday entertainment for the family would be to promenade along the sea front dressed in our best clothes.

only for hokey-pokey men. Rude boys used to shout at these men: 'Hokey-pokey a penny a lump, Enough to make the donkey jump.'

We were never allowed to spend money here on Sundays, although on weekdays we spent part of our penny a week pocket money here, a farthing at a time.

Neither did we go to the beach on Sundays. Our Sunday mornings were spent going for a walk along the seafront with father. We promenaded here with hundreds of other folk all dressed up in their 'Sunday best'.

The ladies, beautifully dressed, all wore buttonholes of fresh flowers, either fixed to their coats or muffs. The gentlemen in smart tailored suits also sported buttonholes. The whole of the seafront from the Palace Pier westwards to the Hove lawns was a veritable fashion parade.

My memory seems to think that the ladies wore palma violets and the gentlemen carnations or roses. Outside the Grand Hotel a flower seller, wearing a large white apron and a hat with flowers on it, sat by the side of a large basket of buttonholes. She did a brisk business.

My father, who was a shopkeeper, had on his Sunday best suit and wore a bowler hat. This he raised, and gave a slight bend, whenever he passed one of his lady customers.

My sister and myself were turned out in our Sunday best frock or coat, beneath which were two petticoats. One made of flannel with buttonhole scallops around the hem, and the other a white cotton one, stiffly starched, with the embroidery around the bottom goffered. This was done with a hot goffering iron which was similar to a pair of old fashioned hair-waving tongs. In the summer we wore white cotton gloves and, in the winter, short kid ones which we had to blow into when we took them off.

The highlight of the walk was to hang over the railing above the fishmarket, and listen to the Salvation Army down on the 'hard'. But, what we waited for expectantly, was 'the penny on the drum' which took place at the end of the service.

The big drum was turned flat, and listeners were invited to throw a penny on the drum. After a short interval, the pennies were counted and then would come the call to those standing up on the top parade: 'Now then, only another penny, or tuppence', as the case might have been, 'to make 10s.'

This brought a few more pennies. Then came the cry: 'Only two more pennies to make 11s'. And so it went on, our excitement rising higher and higher as the pennies descended. We kept our penny until the last, hoping to keep the bidding going. Sometimes, in the height of the season, the collection reached the colossal sum of £1.

Our home was not so strict as some. We were allowed to play with our toys indoors, but never to take them out on Sunday. Not even a doll.

No needlework or knitting was allowed either.

Suet for Sussex

AN old saying in Sussex, often quoted when the subject of suet pudding comes up, is: 'Them as eats most broth gets "ball", them as eats most "ball" gets most meat.'

'Ball', was plain suet crust rolled into a ball and cooked in a cloth, and when it came to table looked like a ball.

Up to the second decade of this century a suet pudding of some kind came to table in many homes every day; in fact, suet pudding is, or was, what batter pudding is to the Yorkshireman.

My grandfather, who was one of those who ate it every day, used to say that the best puddings were made with mutton suet. Perhaps this is the reason for their popularity in Sussex. Certainly the huge flocks of sheep that roamed the Downs would have meant that there was always a plentiful supply of suet.

Why the puddings were made in the shape of a ball, was of course due to the method of cooking in former days. In many cottages the whole dinner had to be cooked in a large oval-shaped iron pot over an open fire, and the balls were more easily fitted into them. The vegetables in net bags were hung around the ball.

Drip pudding always accompanied the joint. This is a plain suet roly-poly boiled for about an hour. It is then taken out and cut into slices of about three-quarters of an inch. These are laid in the fat underneath the joint for a few minutes to catch the drips from the roast – delicious!

At Eartham, in West Sussex, I was told recently by a member in the audience to which I was speaking, that her family liked to have sultanas added to their drip. When I said I did not fancy that, she replied, 'I guess you eat apple sauce with roast pork so why not drip pudding with sultanas?'

'Swimmers', were a great joy when I stayed with my grandmother. She would make me one for my 'elevenses'. Just to think of them takes me back to a cottage garden, with me and my sister sitting on little wooden stools, pulling apart a swimmer floating in butter and a spoonful of brown sugar with an old-fashioned three-pronged fork.

To make swimmers:
roll a piece of suet dough out to about half an inch thick.
Cut into rounds the size of a saucer.
Drop them into boiling water and cook quickly for about fifteen minutes.
Remove with a skimmer (a large spoon with holes in it, that is used to lift out vegetables cooked in the iron pot).
Fork the tops and add a dollop of butter and a spoonful of brown sugar.

In the days when a countryman's wages were low, the pudding was 'hard dick'. This was a roly-poly made without suet. My mother used to tell of a conversation she overheard between two men sitting in the shade of a hedge, and opening up their dinner bags: 'What be got for dinner today then Billy?' 'Hard pudding and pork again, today. Hard pudding and pork.'

Hard pudding, or, hard dick, as it was often called, was made by mixing a cupful of plain flour to a dough with enough water and a pinch of salt into a light dough. This was set in a warm place for an hour to two. It was then tied into a cloth and boiled for about twenty minutes.

Hard dick, along with an onion or a piece of cheese, was the midday meal of many a man. It was probably this pudding that W. D. Parish, was referring to when in his *Dictionary of Sussex Dialect* he states 'he considered that pudding was the cause of all the complaints that Sussex men were subject to'. He should have had a good idea about this. He was vicar of Selmeston in East Sussex from 1863 to 1904. He was wont to say that the first symptom of old age in Sussex, was when a man said he could not get his pudding 'to set' i.e. be digested. He knew then that he was on his way out of this world.

It is said that Cornish women put everything but the devil inside a pasty. Well, Sussex women do the same inside a suet crust. In coaching days many inns became famous for puddings they served. The Jolly Tanner's Inn at Staplefield, then known as The Dun Cow, was famous for its rabbit puddings, which they served daily, all the time there was an 'R' in the month. Rabbits, in my young days, were never sold in May, June, July or August. The aroma from a rabbit pudding on a cold day must have been a very welcome smell to coach passengers as they arrived at the inn for a 20-minute lunch-time stop.

Mrs. Godley, whose roots went deep down into Sussex soil, was a neighbour of mine for many years. She could remember things that happened in the 1890s, and had many interesting stories to tell of the way of old Sussex folk. One of these stories was about her grandparents, who, when she was a child kept the Green Man Inn, at Horsted Keynes. At Christmas time, when the money left in 'The Club' was paid out to members, her grandmother served an individual steak and kidney pudding made in a cloth to each member. She cooked them in a large old-fashioned stone copper, in which the weekly wash was done.

Today the thought of eating singing birds is abhorrent, but it is not so long since sparrows and larks, when in season, could be seen on every poulterer's slab. I can remember seeing sparrows in a large poulterer's in Market Street, Brighton. The 1914 edition of the famous *Mrs Beeton* contains recipes for cooking these little birds: in fact, she quotes that larks were then selling for 3 shillings a dozen.

Some years ago two elderly ladies who said they were the children of a Brighton fisherman in the first decade of this century told me about how their father, when the sea was too rough for him to take his boat out, would go off to the hills beyond Patcham, with a net to catch sparrows. He did this at night and when he returned in the early morning all the family were called upon to pluck and draw the tiny creatures.

When prepared, the birds were threaded in sixes on to a wooden meat skewer, sprinkled with flour and put into a basket on top of a clean white cloth. The two little girls had then to take them to a local poulterer, who bought them for threepence a skewer.

Apparently there was quite a demand for sparrows, and a sparrow pudding was considered to be a great delicacy. *The Sussex Recipe Book*, contains an account of a lark pudding that was made by Arthur Blunden, a one-time landlord of the King's Head at East Hoathly, for a shooting lunch given by Colonel Mardon.

The modern young women raise their hands in horror whenever the old suet puddings are discussed, and say what a bad diet this was. What they forget, however, is that in those days the average family did not eat the rich fare of today. There was no money for cream cakes and such like. It was never bread and butter and jam. You ate plain bread with jam, and plain bread with cheese.

The Last Plough Oxen

WHAT a wonderful sight it was in my childhood to see a team of four oxen ploughing the Sussex farmland. In the 1920s oxen were still ploughing at East Dean, in East Sussex. I saw them at work, and what is more I bought a penny postcard showing them at work, in the local shop-cum-post office.

This team is thought to be the last working ox team in Sussex. The team belonged to Major Harding, a gentleman farmer of Birling Manor Farm. He, however, kept them more as a curiosity than as an economical proposition.

I have met many people who have told me of their memories of the ox teams. At Rodmell W.I., the daughter of the man who drove the last ox team at Exeat Farm said when she was a child she had to act as 'ox-boy' for her father.

Her job was to walk in front of the team with a goad, a long thin pole, and when her father shouted 'stop' or 'go', or 'turn left' or 'turn right', as the case may be, she had to touch a certain ox lightly with the goad.

The animal obeyed immediately, and all the rest of the team went with him. Woe betide, she said, if she touched the wrong ox and it turned left instead of right! When ploughing,

TEAM OF OXEN PLOUGHING ON THE DOWNS. 562.

There were teams of oxen ploughing the Sussex farmland right up to the 1920s.

the four nearside animals walked in the last furrow, and their companions trod beside them on the hard unploughed land.

The men who worked with oxen were very knowledgeable, like their fellow ploughmen were with horses. Frank Wooler had an ox team on High-and-Over Hill, in the Cuckmere Valley, near Seaford. His widow who came to live near me, and who died at the age of 94 in 1966, told me many a tale about the ways of plough oxen. A team was generally made up of eight oxen, although ten were sometimes used when ploughing a steep piece of downland.

The oxen worked in pairs and were chosen as nearly of a size as possible so that the heavy yolks would be level. Mrs. Wooler said that all the pairs had names of one or two syllables, such as Rock and Ruby. When her husband called one name both of the pair would respond, so that if he called 'Rock' when the whole team were resting, Rock would jump up and Ruby with him, and they would stand side by side ready to be harnessed.

It would appear that this was the general practice for naming oxen. The *West Sussex Gazette*, in 1912, published the report of a sale of two teams of four oxen at Chichester. The first team was named Frost and Fairman, and Rock and Ruby. The other team consisted of Turk and Tiger, and Lark and Linnet.

E. O. Mitchell, writing in the *Sussex County Magazine* for 1932, says a ditty known at Mocketts farm at Meads Place, Eastbourne, where his father was foreman went as follows:

'Lark and Gore go before
Flute and Fiddle in the middle
Turk and Tiger go behind
Broad-horn and Buttersnout pull the plough out.'

The shoeing of these great heavy beasts was quite an undertaking. First the animal had to be thrown onto its back on the soft grass, in order that the blacksmith could proceed to fasten on the shoes. These were half-moon shaped pieces of iron known as 'queues'.

The first thing the blacksmith did when he arrived at a farm was to send to the kitchen for a piece of fat pork. This was used as a pin-cushion to hold the sharp nails with triangular heads that were used for shoeing. This also gave the nails a slight greasing.

When the shoeing was over there was much competition for the piece of pork. This was a coveted prize as in those hard times it could be made into a dinner for a whole family.

In *Life on a Sussex Farm in the Sixties* by Maude Robinson, which is an account of her young life on her father's farm at Saddlescombe, near the Devil's Dyke, there is a photo of an ox lying on the ground ready for shoeing. A little ox-boy sits on its massive neck to prevent it struggling.

Miss Pelling, a friend of mine who lives in Brighton, told me proudly that the little ox-boy in the photograph is her father and the ox driver looking on is her grandfather. Unfortunately she is not old enough to have any memories of the oxen.

In the early days most Sussex farmers used the red breed of oxen. Later, however, the black curly polled, wide-horned Pembrokes became popular. These black and white oxen at Piddinghoe became known as 'magpies' which gave rise to the well-known saying: 'Piddinghoe, where they shoe the magpies'.

But alas, neither breed of oxen can be seen working on the land today.

The Custom of Bendin-In

THE mackerel fishing in Brighton is now almost a thing of the past now but I can remember when the coming of the mackerel was eagerly awaited all along the Sussex coast.

The mackerel were usually punctual in their coming. At Brighton it was around the end of April and the beginning of May; in fact, the fishermen were always happiest if they arrived on May Day itself.

The shoals would be watched for and could sometimes be seen quite a long way off. Up to 1896, the old custom of Bendin-In was kept up. Jack (Dapper) Twaites, who had a boat on the Bedford Street beach in my schooldays, would tell us about how he took part in the custom of Bendin-In, or rather, as he called it 'bread-and-cheese-and-beer day'.

The custom took place on the day that the boats set sail for the first mackerel catch. It was a feast provided by the Masters of each boat for the men, their wives and their children. There were two beaches on which the parties were held. One was the beach in front of the Old Ship Hotel, and the other was the Bedford Street beach.

One of the first tasks Dapper had to perform on the day he started in the fishing trade was to do the shopping for the

An engraving of the mackerel fishermen conducting a fish auction on the beach.

feast for the Master of the boat to whom he was apprenticed. This he had to cart down to the beach. He even told me the price he paid for the bread, cheese and beer. Large loaves cost three-halfpence (old money), round red cheeses weighing two pounds were sixpence halfpenny each, beer cost twopence a pint and gingerpop three-halfpence a pint.

Before the parties began, the nets were bent up into neat concertina shapes and laid out on the beach behind all the people who were taking part in the feast. According to Dapper it was the bent nets that gave the custom its name. He said it should be 'benting it'. But he was mistaken in this. The word was probably derived from Benediction and the nets were folded thus for the vicar to give them his blessing. However, some think its origins go further back than this to the days when our pagan ancestors made a libation to the gods who looked after the fishing, because the Anglo-Saxon word for ask or supplication is 'Biddy-Ben'.

What is certain, however, is that in later centuries it meant benediction. The Vicar of Brighton used to come down and give his blessing to the men and nets before they set sail. Hence the folded nets. No doubt in the days before the Reformation the nets would have been sprinkled with holy water.

The second part of the ceremony took place when the mackerel were caught. Mackerel nets were very large and long and they hung down in sea like gates. One side of the nets had little barrels attached to them to keep them afloat and to show where they were set.

When the last of the barrels went overboard, the men took off their hats and bowed their heads in prayer, while the Master repeated the 'Watch, barrel, watch prayer.' The prayer is thought to be old. Some people think it might have been first taught to the fishermen by the monks of St. Bartholomew's Priory, whose land went down to the edge of the cliff just above the fishmarket.

On some boats the prayer was repeated line and line about by the Master and his men. On the boat where Dapper started work, the Master repeated the prayer. It went:

'Watch, barrel, watch!
Mackerel for to catch.
White may they be like blossom on a tree.
God sends thousands, one, two, three.
Some by their heads and some by their tails.
God sends thousands and never fails.'

When the prayer ended the Master said, 'God Almighty, send us a blessing it is to be hoped' or 'For what we are about to receive, Amen.' To this the men all shouted 'Seize, Haul'. If this was not said then bad luck in the form of the nets getting tangled, or the catch being lost, would surely follow.

In pre-Christian days, Brighton fishermen were probably throwing bread and cheese into the sea at the beginning of the mackerel fishing to placate the gods who looked after the fishing.

Alas! gone are the days when thousands of mackerel jumped and thrashed furiously about on the beaches here. In recent years, mackerel have deserted the Sussex beaches and with the end of the mackerel fishing fleets, so another old custom of Sussex is gone too.

Brighton's First Motor Trials

EVERY year on the first Saturday in September Motor Trials are held on the Madeira Road, which runs by the side of the beaches at Brighton. It is done in memory of the first Motor Trials ever to be held which took place on this self same track in July 1905. The event lasted for a week.

There cannot be a lot of people alive who remember it, but I am one who saw it. I was only five years old at the time, but my memories of it are still vivid. My home at that time was almost opposite the entrance to the stables of the New Steine Hotel, now the New Steine Mansions, a block of flats on the corner of Devonshire Place and St James Street.

In those days there were few garages about; in fact, I doubt if there were any at all in Brighton. The owners of motor cars were men of money. They were then the rich man's plaything, and hotels allowed them to park their cars in the stables. The Old Ship Hotel used the stables for parking cars right up to 1910. In that year it was found that the arch of the stables was too small and low so it had to be removed. The removal of the beam over the entrance is a little bit of history, for this arch is believed to be a carved beam from *The Surprise*, the boat on which Charles II escaped to France in 1651 after the battle of Worcester, during the Civil Wars. The owner of *The Surprise* Nicholas Tettersell, bought the Old Ship inn, later hotel, with money he received as a reward for this. The beam is now in Brighton Museum.

From the window of my home I could watch the cars coming in and out. I do not remember anything about the cars except that they were small and made a terrible noise.

The town went mad with excitement. Thousands of spectators came to the town, some daily but many to stay. All the hotels and boarding houses were full, the shopkeepers did a good trade and everyone was happy. I remember the draper who lived opposite, one morning, calling across to my father 'That is going to spoil your carrot trade', as he pointed to the motor cars coming out of the stables. (Apparently father did a good trade with the stable lads who looked after the horses.)

People were standing two or three deep all along the top railings from The Aquarium to Dukes Mound. All the while I was watching I remember being very frustrated by my mother holding on to the back of my dress as I leaned through the railings because she was sure the railings would give way under the great pressure on them by people leaning forward every time a car came along the bottom road.

A charge was made for people to stand on the middle walk, or terrace for viewing, just as it is to this day. Because the Electric Railway had to stop while the trials were being run, Mr. Volk of Volk's Electric Railway, made up for his loss of revenue by erecting some sort of platform on top of the Paston Place station. I am not sure what it was but I remember seeing people sitting on chairs on the roof.

No one but officials were allowed on the Madeira Road, but hundreds of people walked along the beaches from the Aquarium and then climbed over Volk's railway track. Here between the track and the railings of the Madeira Road they were squashed together four or five deep.

The start of the race, or trials, was from a little way beyond the bottom of Dukes Mound, about where the Twitten leads up to the top of the Mound, to a spot about level with the steps that lead down from the top at Atlingworth Street. The

Brighton's first Motor Trials in July 1905.

cars taking part in the trials had to line up on the slope that leads down to the road just before The Marina.

Although these were the first trials, it was not the first motor event that took place at Brighton. On the 14th November, 1896, a damp, dismal and foggy day, according to the report in a local paper, the day of the Motor Car had arrived. On this day the first London to Brighton run was made. So great was the interest that people lined the London road from Westminster Bridge to Streatham.

It is commonplace today to see motor cars lining both sides of the streets in many towns, but when I was born there was hardly a car to be seen. Small wonder then that the excitement of these first Brighton Motor Trials made such an impact on my memory when I was a little girl.

Harvest Home Fare

TODAY much of the traditional fare that at one time was connected with harvest appears to have completely been forgotten. How many people in Sussex now make a pumpkin pie, or a warden pie? Both of these in my childhood were regular dishes for 'afters'.

My grandmother considered that a pumpkin pie was a delicacy. She used to make one every year from a pumpkin that she grew specially in her garden.

Some people still make them but perhaps only people with old-fashioned taste buds really enjoy them. They are much too spicy for modern young folk, who prefer to use wine to flavour a dish rather than spice.

A Sussex pumpkin pie is far different to the pie that is still popular in the United States of America at harvest time. A few years ago I was visiting Kentucky at harvestide and pumpkins were everywhere. A large or small pumpkin rested on the doorstep of many houses, and a bunch of corn-on-the-cob was fixed to the front door.

In the stores there were counters full of golden cardboard pumpkins which were sold to parents for their children, who went around with them at Hallowe'en calling on neighbours who put in some sweets or a 'cookie'. No one could forget that harvest had arrived or forget to make a pumpkin pie.

Our Sussex Pumpkin pie was very different to the American one which is rather like a baked custard. My grand-mother's pumpkin pie was made from a recipe that she had inherited from her mother, Mary Ann Floate, who was born in Clematis Cottage, Washington, between Storrington and Steyning, in or around 1822.

Grandmother's Pumpkin Pie:
Fill a pie dish with diced pumpkin, that has been boiled in a little water until tender, and diced cooking apples.
Add some washed currants, a liberal helping of moist brown sugar, a big pinch of mixed spice and ground ginger. Souse well with lemon juice.
Top with good short pastry and bake in a moderate, to slow oven, for about 40 minutes.
Lift the lid and pour in three or four tablespoonfuls of thick rich cream, and serve at once.

Harvest Pumpkin Custards:
Boil one pound of diced pumpkin to a pulp with a little water and sugar.
When cold beat in a knob of butter, a pinch of ground ginger, a pinch of cinnamon, two well beaten eggs and a pint of milk.
Continue to beat for two or three minutes.
Line a pie plate with puff pastry.
Bake for a few minutes to set the pastry. Three parts fill with pumpkin mixture and bake in a moderate oven for about 35 minutes.

These pumpkin custards were much more like the harvest pies made in the U.S.A. When pumpkins were not available people used a ripe marrow instead. The only difference being that the colour was not so good and the flavour not so strong.

Warden Pies were made with warden pears. They are almost unknown today, but up to Edwardian times, when fruit in the winter months was limited to apples and pears, they were very popular. Wardens have had a long history. They were known in Saxon times. In fact, their name is made up of two Anglo-Saxon words: 'Wear' and 'den', meaning long keeping.

In Brighton at that time, the Pavilion Creamery, a high-class restaurant just east of the south gateway of the Royal Pavilion, in the winter months always had a china decorated bowl full of stewed wardens in the centre of their window, with a bowl of rich thick cream alongside.

Wardens were not soft like the modern stewing pear. They were quite hard when cooked and needed good teeth to eat them. They seem now to have completely disappeared from the shops. The last time I saw any was in a greengrocers' shop in the centre of Ditchling village.

To make a warden pie:
Peel the pears and quarter them, then simmer them in sweetened water for about two, to two and a half hours. By this time they should be tender and have turned a pale pink colour.
Leave them to get cold.
Meanwhile line the edge of a pie dish with thin pastry.
Fill the dish with the pears, add a little lemon juice, and a wineglassful of claret or port wine.
Top with pastry and bake. When serving lift the lid and gently spoon in two or three tablespoonsful of rich thick cream.

In Tudor times, if Shakespeare is to be believed, the pies were also flavoured with saffron. In *The Winter's Tale*, he makes Clown say to himself what he has to buy. 'I must have saffron to colour the Warden pies.'

Seed or Seedy cakes were another essential item of the harvest feast. Caraway seeds have long had a reputation for being able to give strength to the eater. Therefore one can imagine that the farmer's wife baked great batches of seed cakes, for strength was certainly what a man needed for getting in the harvest, in the days before farm machinery had been invented. The seeds were also said to be able to prevent thieves taking things away, so it may be that the farmer's wife provided seed cakes as a way of binding together the farmer and his men.

To make a seedy cake:
Rub six ounces of good beef dripping into one and a half pounds of self-raising flour.
Add a pinch of salt, a teaspoonful of caraway seeds, a little chopped candied peel, pinch of nutmeg, and sugar to taste.
Whisk the whites of two eggs, and beat the yolks.
Stir these slowly into the dry ingredients along with enough milk to make a soft dough, and then beat well.
Turn the mixture into a well-greased cake tin. Bake in a moderate oven for about one and a half hours.

Some farmers' wives preferred to make seedy bread at harvest. For this three ounces of lard, a teaspoonful of caraway seeds and a little fine sugar was kneaded into a pound of bread dough. Bake in a hot oven for about 20 minutes, either as rolls or in a bread loaf tin. Seed cakes today appear to have gone quite out of fashion with modern folk, but as children it was very popular with us; in fact, it alternated with plum cake for serving at Sunday teatime. What a pity it is that these traditional foods of Harvest time no longer grace our tables.

Sussex Truffle
and Morel Hunters

IN the 1920s when walking in The Slipes, a small copse on
the side of Washington bostel, I came across a form of fungi
which was new to me.

John Butcher, a local man, whose knowledge of country
lore could not be faulted, said it was a morel. With a chuckle,
he added 'They do say as though these morels never grow no
more once anyone looks on them.'

He then went on to tell how when he was a boy – he was
born in the 1870s – morels were very plentiful. The villagers
gathered them by the basketful and threaded them onto
string. These strings they sold to local market gardeners who
in turn took the strings of morel to Brighton or Worthing
markets. Here the morels were quickly snapped up, chiefly by
chefs from the seaside hotels or cooks who worked in the big
houses. It would appear that the addition of a morel gave an
epicurean flavour to many a dish.

Now, not only have morels disappeared from Sussex soil,
but all knowledge of them has disappeared. Why? Could it be
that the old belief that morels do not like being looked at is
responsible?

Certainly this is thought to be the reason for the disappear-

A *woodcut of a Sussex truffle hunter which appeared in* The Penny Magazine *in 1838.*

ance of the truffle, which a century ago was so plentiful in Sussex that men made a living by hunting for them with dogs or pigs.

Truffles, those exotic underground fungi, sometimes called ground mushrooms, are generally thought of as being fare only for gourmets and wealthy folk. This, however, was not always the case. A century or so ago truffles were still to be found in Sussex. *The Penny Magazine* for March 10th 1838, contains a woodcut of a Sussex truffle hunter. He is enveloped in a large round frock (smock) that reaches down to his knees. On his head is a tall hard hat, and under his arm is a long handled spade. At his feet are two shaggy haired dogs. One is a poodle and the other a French barbet. Both are looking expectantly at something he is holding out to them in his hand. He is standing under a beech tree on the Downs and southwards in the far distance can be seen the coastline and the sea.

This man made a living by hunting truffles on the hills of Eartham, Slindon and Goodwood with dogs. Truffles when first gathered look like large black pickled walnuts, powdered with cocoa — in fact just like the chocolate truffles sold by confectioners.

In England they were found under beech trees, but in France they are sought for under oak trees. They grow at any distance from just below the surface to some seven or eight inches underground. When ripe, they give off a very strong scent and it is this smell that the dogs are taught to find.

Truffle dogs when fully trained are exceedingly clever. They would sniff around until they got the scent of a truffle and then get it out quite cleanly. If, however, a truffle was deep down this was the time for the spade to be used to help them dig the truffle out.

W. D. Daniels, in *Rural Sports* 1807, writes of a dog which went out with his truffle hunting owner in Amsbury Park, who leapt over the hedge surrounding the park and ran to a beech tree, some hundred yards away, where he began to dig and before long he was back with a twelve ounce truffle in his mouth completely unharmed.

77

Another truffle hunter was William Leech of Patching. Horsfield, in his *History of Sussex* published in 1835, says that Leech used pigs for hunting truffles. Leech had been living in the West Indies, and had such a love of truffles that he brought home with him several specially trained pigs. He decided he would make his home where the best truffles grew. Accordingly he spent four years travelling from Land's End to the mouth of the Thames in his search. The place where truffles were at their best and most plentiful he decided was in the woods near the village of Patching, that lies to the north of Goring. Here he settled and remained there for the rest of his life.

Leech's method of hunting with pigs was the same as is still used in some parts of France. A cord is tied around the hind leg of the pig and when it begins to root, the cord is given a tug which pulls the pig away while the truffle is dug out. This is necessary, for unless the hunter is quick the pig will gobble up the truffle.

An oft repeated tale is told to visitors in Périgord of a sow who became very clever. She would sniff and root under an oak tree where she knew there were no truffles, and while her owner was busy digging, she went quickly to another tree where she knew there was a truffle and before you could say 'Jack Robinson', she had rooted up and swallowed a nice fat one!

A lady living in Lewes said that back in the 1920s she knew a man who used to find truffles under beech trees growing on the hill below Firle beacon who used neither dogs or pigs. Apparently the man would lie full length on the ground when he came across a small mound and sniff. If he got the scent of a truffle he dug and found one.

Today, men who love good food, go to Périgueux, the citadel of the truffle to eat pâté de foie gras, truffle omelettes, truffle sous la cendre and other local specialities.

Sussex once had its own specialities to tempt people into the inns. M. K. Samuelson, in *A Sussex Recipe Book*, published in 1938, says: 'I have read of a Patcham truffle pie, but have been unable to obtain the recipe.' In view of Patching's former fame for truffles, I surmise this may have been 'A Patching Truffle Pie', made according to an 1810 recipe which is similar to the famous Strasburg pies, beloved by gourmets.

I obtained the recipe from an 1810 cookery book written by Francis Collingworth and John Woolworth, cooks to the Crown and Anchor Inn, in the Strand, London.

The original recipe is rather lengthy but in modern speech it is as follows:

Truffle Pie:
Chop and cook one pound of veal, half a pound of fat ham, four ounces lean ham, six fat goose livers and a shallot.
Add four ounces marrow (scooped from the centre of a marrow bone), chopped parsley, thyme and seasoning.
Pound the mixture until all is 'well incorporated' and leave till cold.
Meanwhile make a raised pie. Three parts fill with the mixture, and top with sliced truffles.
Put pastry lid on and bake in an oven made 'very hot with faggots'.
When about to serve lift the lid and pour in a glass of madeira.

No one today appears to have an authentic reason as to why truffles have disappeared from the Sussex woods and hills. Some people put it down to the high prices that were paid for truffles, or the hills being overworked. But it is much more likely that it is due to the spread of population.

In a nature talk on the B.B.C. some time ago the panel who were discussing truffles and their disappearance all agreed that truffles will only grow under very old beech trees, where the roots are undisturbed. So it looks as though the old folk are right in their belief that morels and truffles do not like being looked at.

Turning the Cup Over

TURNING the Cup Over is an old Sussex custom that used to be carried out at the end of harvest time. In fact, it was a part of the Harvest Home Supper.

Just when the custom started of the farmers providing a Harvest Home feast for all employees is hard to say, but from old pictures and the names of country dances, etc., they must certainly go back to at least Tudor times. The feasts were always celebrated with a lot of eating and drinking. Arthur Beckett, editor of the old *Sussex Magazine*, who loved all things pertaining to Sussex, wrote in one of his books about the county that the Harvest Home was 'an event for heavy feeding, curious songs and big drinking'.

On the smaller farms, up to a century ago, the Harvest Home feasts took place in the farm barn or kitchen, on the day the last load was carried in.

Many years ago, an old man told me about the harvest suppers he remembered when he was 'in House' on a farm in East Sussex, as a young man. 'In house' meant that he lived in. As soon as 'the last load' had been unpitched the announcement that 'supper is ready' would be made. In a very short time the carters, farm servants and casual labourers (these were treated the same as the yearly servants), with hands and faces as clean as soap and water could make them, would come to the barn and arrange themselves around the

food laden table, in order of precedence. And what a sight it
was!

When the meal was over, the table was cleared, and a large
milking-pan, scoured until it looked like silver and filled with
foaming ale was put in the centre, in front of the chairman,
generally the head shepherd. This man stood in front of the
pail and into it he dipped a horn-cup. The cup was passed to
the man on his left who took the cup on the crown of his hard
hat. No handling was allowed so he had to take great care.
Holding the brim of the hat in both hands, he steadied it well
before beginning to drink. As soon as he began to drink his
fellow workers began to sing:

> 'I've been to Plymouth and I've been to Dover,
> I've been rambling all the world over,
> Over and over and over and over.
> Drink up your liquor and turn the cup over,
> Over and over and over and over.
> The liquor's drunk up and the cup is turned over.'

While the song was being sung the drinker had to raise the
horn-cup to his lips, drink the ale without spilling any, toss
the cup high into the air, and catch it inside the hat before the
men had reached the last line. If this was not done properly,
the singers altered the last line to 'The liquor's drunk'd up
and the cup ain't turned over'. The man who failed had then
to start all the procedure over again and pay threepence. And,
of course, the more times he missed, the less chance he had of
doing it.

This song may have been exported from Sussex to the New
World, for in Kentucky, U.S.A., I discovered a song that used
to be sung there at children's parties. It was a kind of singing
game. The words are:

> 'I've been to Harlem and I've been to Boston,
> I've been sailing all the world over,
> Over and over and over and over
> Drink up your barley juice and turn the glass over.'

81

My shepherd's horn cup, which must have often been used in the ceremony of 'Turning the Cup Over'.

More surprisingly, it may even have been taken to West Africa by a Sussex emigrant. Some years ago, I received a letter from a lady who had been schoolteaching in West Africa. She wrote that when she was leaving the school and returning to England, the girls, to honour her and say goodbye, sang in English the verse 'I've been to Plymouth etc.' She was unable to discover how they had learned it.

I am the possessor of an old horn cup that in all likelihood was once used to turn the cup over. It was given to me by the daughter of a Sussex shepherd who once walked the hills at the back of Brighton behind his flock. It is a most treasured possession. In shape it is like a large tumbler, and it is made out of a bull's horn. It is quite heavy and holds nearly half a pint of liquid. The bottom appears to have been filled with a round of wood which inside is covered with some sort of putty substance. It is really very lovely and the texture of the outside is beautifully smooth. Every time I handle it I wish it could speak, for what tales it would tell of those Harvest Home customs of long ago.

The Rise of the Scallop

'FINE fresh scallops!' was the cry of Brighton fishermen as they pushed their barrows through the streets in the early years of this century.

In those days scallops were considered to be the poor man's food. I have talked to many elderly people who remembered, when they were young, that families would sit down to a great dish of scallops. In the early 1890s they were cheaper still. A Hastings man when telling me about how plentiful they were, said that his mother would sit the family down around a well scrubbed wooden table, turn the cooked scallops into the centre, give each child a hunk of bread and leave them to get on with it. This, he assured me, was the best way of eating scallops as you then tasted nothing but scallops.

My mother used to tell how when she was a child at the end of the 19th century, boats loaded with scallops, mussels and other fish came up the river from Newhaven to Lewes. They anchored by some steps by the side of the bridge in the Cliff High Street. When this happened, Mr. English, the town crier, who had a cutler's business on the corner of English's Passage, would don his official hat, and come around the streets crying: 'O Yes! O Yes! O Yes! Just arrived and now selling at the Bridge, Lewes. Fine fresh, scallops, twopence a dozen. Full roed mackerel 16 a shilling.'

On hearing this cry, grandmother would give my mother (then a child) a shilling and a basket and, along with one of her brothers or sisters, she would set off for the bridge. The shilling bought five dozen scallops, and the filled basket was so heavy that it was as much as the two children could carry between them.

Scallops were almost unknown in hotels or restaurants before 1818. At that time *The Brighton Ambulator*, a paper published principally for the visitors which were beginning to come to the town, when enumerating the many kinds of fish caught off Brighton, ends the paragraph with: 'There is also a delicious shell fish caught here called an escollop, but little known in London markets; and which, for its nutritive qualities, and richness of flavour, has scarcely its equal. The season for this delicacy is early in the spring.'

In spite of this glowing advertisement for scallops, their popularity did not become widespread until some ninety or so years later. And since then the scallop has gone up and up in the world, until it is now rich man's fare.

Perhaps it is motor transport that is responsible for the rise to fame of the scallop. Certainly this may have had something to do with it, because with no quick transport and no refrigeration fish from the coast could go bad before it got to the markets inland.

In my childhood 'queenies', a small kind of scallop, were hawked around the streets on fishbarrows. I have not seen any for years until just recently, I saw some in a Brighton shop. They were displayed on the slab of a fishmonger's shop, at an exhorbitant price. I asked the fishmonger why they were so scarce, and he said, that they had become a great delicacy in France, and the French were buying them up at a price far higher than the English were prepared to pay. 'Queenies' were always considered to be a great delicacy by local people, and as soon as the cry 'Fresh! Queenies! Fresh!' was heard there would be a rush as women came out of their houses armed with plates and baskets. The fishermen used to eat them raw, and often the man selling them would pick one or two choice ones up from his barrow, prise them open and tip the contents down his throat like an oyster.

I have been told of a small scallop called a 'chinkerberry ring', but I have never seen one. These are said to have got their name from a particular spot in the sea off Worthing, overlooked by Chanctonbury Ring, a ring of trees on the top of a hill north of Worthing. I wonder if these could have been 'queenies' under a different name?

People who are descended from one of the fishing families of Sussex hold that scallops should be cooked in a simple fashion, saying that a dish should taste of what it is supposed to be. They don't agree with all the 'dollying up' of scallops with herbs, wine, etc.

When scallops were cheap the popular way was to cook them gently in water for about ten minutes. When cool they were dusted with flour and fried in great batches. Some people dipped the scallops in egg and breadcrumbs before frying. Another way is to simmer the scallops for ten to fifteen minutes, according to the size. These are drained and chopped and reheated in a white sauce, or a parsley sauce.

My mother always served them in their shells. The shell was buttered and sprinkled with fine breadcrumbs. Spoonfuls of the scallops in white sauce were put into the shells which were topped with a layer of breadcrumbs. Then with a few small knobs of butter put here and there they were popped under the grill until the tops were an appetising brown colour. I can picture them now. They *were* delicious!

The Wassail Bowl

'Wassail, Wassail, All over the town
Our toast it is white and our ale it is brown,
Our bowl is made of the good ashen tree;
With the wassailing bowl we'll drink to thee.

Love and joy come to you and to your wassail too;
And God bless you, and send you a happy New Year.'

SONGS similar to this were once heard on the last day of
December in homes and inns all over the county. The early
wassailers went around with a be-ribboned drinking bowl,
made either of wood or china, or in some cases silver.

First the bowls were taken around empty, and in return for
a song and good wishes, the wassailers begged the ingredients
for making the wassail drink.

Having obtained the wherewithal to fill the bowl, the drink
was prepared and once again the bowl went around the
streets. This time money was collected for a sip of the drink.
It was considered very unlucky to refuse to drink.

At the Red Lion Inn, which lies in the shadow of Old
Shoreham Church, a wassailing custom was kept up on New
Year's Day as late as 1883. The custom was called 'The
Bushel', and the *Sussex Daily News* of January 5th that year
contains an account of it.

A bushel corn measure decorated with green paper, flowers and Christmas greenery was filled to the brim with foaming ale, so that it looked like a huge cauliflower. A man known as 'the baler' ladled the ale out into large glasses with a pint measure.

This man had the privilege of drinking direct from the measure whenever he felt like it. Every customer who came to the inn on this night was entitled to a drink from the bushel free of charge. The brewers who owned the inn supplied the liquor that filled the bushel and kept it filled.

Right up to the early years of this century, where a New Year's party was being held, Sussex folk kept up the custom of the Wassail bowl. As the evening began to approach the hour of 12 o'clock, a large bowl, filled with hot spiced ale would be brought in, on top of which floated 'lamb's wool' – the white fluffy inside of roasted apples, which looked like lamb's wool. This was placed in a central spot.

Everyone then formed up around the bowl, and began to move around it clockwise, singing and stirring the ale at the same time. Then the clock struck 12, glasses were filled from the bowl, and one and all wished each other 'good wassail'.

One of the best descriptions of such a wassail bowl must surely be Charles Dicken's recording of the wassail bowl that was at 'Dingley Dell': 'A mighty bowl of wassail; something smaller than an ordinary wash-house copper, in which the hot apples were hissing and bubbling with a rich look and a jolly sound that was perfectly irresistible.'

The liquor that filled many Sussex wassail bowls was called 'Lamb's Wool'. Here is a recipe from the *Sussex Recipe Book* 1937.

'Take eight roasted apples, mash them, and add to them one quart of good old ale; press through a strainer, add half a teaspoonful each of grated ginger and nutmeg, sweeten to taste, make hot, but do not let it boil, and drink hot.'

The word wassail comes from the Anglo-Saxon 'wes-hail'

— to be in health. If tradition can be believed, the word was first used in Britain just over the border of East Sussex, in Kent. The story goes that when Hengist and Horsa landed here they were made welcome by Vortigern, the king of South Britain, who gave them much land.

Hengist, no doubt, with an eye to the future, sent home for his daughter, the lovely Rowena. When she arrived Hengist gave a feast for Vortigern, and during the meal Rowena entered with a golden cup and, kneeling down before the king, offered him a drink, saying 'wassail'. The king not understanding her, asked what he should reply, and she told him: 'Drinkaile'. The end of the story? In the best tradition, they married and lived happily ever after.

Christmas Fare of Long Ago

IN the early years of this century Christmas tea was a great occasion. Today the family is often so full up with the Christmas dinner, which in many homes is still served at mid-day, that they have no room for Christmas tea.

Teatime on Christmas day in Edwardian times was generally around five o'clock, when the family had had time to go for a walk to let their dinner settle down.

And my, what a spread it was! Sandwiches and cakes of all kinds, with the great centre piece of the Christmas cake, or biscuit as it was always called by my grandmother, in spite of her grandchildren repeatedly telling her that it was a cake, not a biscuit. She would reply with a chuckle 'My mother called it a biscuit and if biscuit was good enough for her it is good enough for me.'

Later, however, I discovered that as a Sussex woman she was correct. Parish, in his *Dictionary of Sussex Dialect* (1875) writes: 'In Sussex the words biscuit and cake interchange their usual meaning.' The writer of the *Cook's Oracle* (1822) also refers to this in a recipe for Christmas cake. She writes 'The goodness of the cake or biscuit depends on it being well baked.'

My father's greengrocery shop shortly before the First World War. It is decked out with a wonderful array of traditional fare for Christmas.

She claimed that the secret for the goodness of her cake was due to the dripping which had come from the joint of beef that had been eaten on Stir-up Sunday. This is the last Sunday in the church's year, when the Collect repeated at Matins begins with the words 'Stir up we beseech Thee, O Lord.' The words of which are said to have been taken by the women in the congregation as a signal that it was time to start preparing for the great Christmas feast. It was really a feast in those days. Someone recently, when looking back on Christmas past said that the modern child has Christmas every day. She was right when you think of Edwardian days!

Much of the fare now connected with Christmas but eaten all the year round did not appear until Christmas in those days. Take oranges for instance. Up to the 1920s oranges were only in season from early December until early April. The only place in the days before refrigeration that sent oranges to England was Spain. At Christmas these were very sour. So much so that we were allowed to poke a hole in the skins and into the hole push a lump of sugar. The juice was then sucked through the sugar. At that time there was no bottled or tinned orange juice, so oranges were definitely a large part of Christmas, and every child hoped to see an orange sticking out of the top of their stocking.

Another fruit enjoyed at Christmas but hardly ever seen today was the medlar. This looks like a large brown rose hip. In fact, the medlar tree (*Mespilus germanica*) belongs to the rose family. The fruit is picked in late autumn, but they are not ready for eating until about Christmas, when they will have softened and the insides look like a rotten apple, with three large pips in the centre. Why this fruit has lost favour is surprising. To my mind medlars are delicious and are far superior to the exotic fruits that we are now persuaded to buy. Medlars could be bought in Brighton as late as the 1950s. As a school girl I bought many a half pint for twopence (old money). The greengrocer would measure them into a tall wooden measure, shaped rather like a jug. When he was in a good mood he would top the measure generously.

Why people with large gardens don't plant medlar trees is a mystery. They are hardy and look lovely in the early summer when covered with blossom. There is a flourishing tree in the garden of Southover Grange, at Lewes, and another in the village of West Dean in East Sussex, on which I look with covetousness.

Perhaps the most important thing, however, was the Christmas Cake. These in the shops today often appear to be of one style, but in the day of the one-man bakery shop, each one tried to outdo the shop along the road. So much so, that on the Sunday before Christmas the window blinds were left up and the cakes put on show for all to see. On the way to Sunday School in Brighton, two such shops had to be passed. One belonged to Mr. Day and the other to Mr. Parish. To these windows we glued our noses and often got late for school.

Both men used completely different designs. Mr. Day, who had a shop in Upper St. James Street, decorated his cakes in a most exciting way. How he did his decorations I have no idea. On top of each cake was a plain sheet of white icing, which had pictures on it that looked as though it had been drawn with a red crayon. There were skating scenes with ladies gliding across the ice with their hands tucked into muffs; children playing at snow-balling; Father Christmas on his sleigh and many others. Mr. Parish iced his cakes in the more conventional manner, but here again the designs were many and varied.

A baker to whom I was talking about this icing of cakes said that the time that would have to be spent on icing original designs would today make the cakes far too costly. Alas! We all have more time than our forefathers but, when it comes to spending it at work, it just cannot be done. What a lot the children of today are missing!

Index

Acknowledgements

Many thanks to the editor of the West Sussex Gazette for permission to print any material of mine that has appeared in his paper.

I am grateful to Mr T. B. Mills for permission to use his photograph of Garland Day at Cowfold, to Tony Wales who kindly loaned his postcards of the Sussex shepherds and The Oxen ploughing for use in my book, and to Tony Tree for all his help with my own photographs.

Lillian Candlin